COMPASS PONY GUI

8. Why Does He Do That?

Text by Barbara Cooper

Illustrations by Maggie Raynor

Series consultant: Valerie Watson
Compass Equestrian

© Compass Equestrian Limited 1996
Setting by HRJ
Origination by Dot Gradations
Printed in England by Westway Offset
ISBN 1 900667 07 X
British Library Cataloguing in Publication Data.
A catalogue record for this book is available from the British Library.

Like cats, dogs, sheep, goats, pigs, donkeys and cattle, ponies and horses are known as 'domestic' animals. This is because they live close to humans.

The first animals to be 'domesticated' (about 14,000 years ago) were dogs, followed later by sheep, pigs, goats, cattle and donkeys. Then about 6000 years ago, nomadic, or wandering, tribesmen on the Asian borders of Europe first decided to round up herds of horses and ponies.

To begin with, they used them for their meat, milk, skins, and dung (which made good fuel for fires).

Then they found that they could use them for riding, carrying loads, and pulling carts or chariots.

Long before ponies and horses became domesticated they lived in the wild, wandering across the vast 'steppes', or grasslands, of eastern Europe and Asia. They were herd animals, living together in large family groups. The world in which they lived was harsh and cruel, and they were hunted both by men and wild beasts.

They had little shelter from rain, snow, wind and sun, and had to keep moving around to find water and fresh grass. In order to survive they had to stay together and help to protect each other.
In their struggle to live they depended not just on their speed but on their senses – of sight, hearing, taste, smell and touch.

For us humans, with our space shuttles and our computers, life has changed a great deal in only *fifty* years, but ponies are still very much the same as they were thousands of years ago.

They are still herd animals. Their senses – especially hearing, sight and smell – are sharper than ours, going back to the time when their ancestors were the hunted and ours were the hunters.

Even the kindest, most gentle, best-behaved pony may surprise you now and again by doing something that you aren't quite expecting – such as snorting, or jumping over a shadow, or shying (swerving suddenly) at a hosepipe or a plastic bag in his path.

A shadow or a plastic bag may remind him of some fierce animal about to jump up at him.

The snort may be caused by the smell of a pig, which ponies don't like – probably because in the past their ancestors were often attacked by wild pigs.

A hosepipe may remind him of a snake.

The 'herd instinct', or the need to be in a family group, is still strong, and when several ponies are in a field together they will always have an order of importance. The 'herd' leader is usually the bossiest (not the biggest, or the oldest) pony; it might be the youngest or a mare. The last pony in the order is usually the most 'laid-back'. When Miss Bossy wants to make sure that she has the best grazing she will put Mr Laid-Back in his place by nipping and pulling faces at him.

Even a stabled pony may be irritable when he is eating, and may kick out if you disturb him: he thinks that you are going to steal his food! This is why you should never try to groom or remove tack from a pony who is having a meal.

When food is being given to ponies in a field it should not be put all in one place, or there will be kicking, biting and jostling as each pony fights for his or her position.

During cold, wet or windy weather, a group of ponies in a field will huddle together to keep each other warm and dry. When they are asleep, there will always be one pony standing on guard.

A herd of wild horses will escape from any kind of danger by running away. For the same reason, when your domesticated pony is frightened he may try to run away – even if you are riding or leading him.

A pony who is with his herd in a field may be very difficult to catch because he doesn't want to leave the others for his human friend, even if you try to bribe him with his favourite tit-bits.

It is because of his herd instinct that a pony can't bear being on his own. Whether he is in a stable or in a field he needs a friend to keep him company. It could be another pony or it could be some other kind of animal.

Two ponies together can become such friends that if they are separated they will be very upset and become thoroughly unsettled.

These are some of the other animals that ponies enjoy making friends with.

Unlike humans, who spend a lot of their time chattering, ponies don't waste their breath making noises at each other (or at *you*) unless they have a good reason.

They neigh – which is a very loud 'hello' – to attract the attention of another pony, or of a human.

They whinny – which is not as loud as a neigh – because they are pleased or are expecting something nice.

They whicker, or nicker – which is a soft, gentle sound – when they are greeting each other nose to nose.

They squeal only when they are having a quarrel with another animal.

As well as sight, hearing, taste, touch and smell, ponies have a 'sixth sense', which humans find very puzzling but sometimes very useful.

If there is danger, a pony will sense it long before you do, and may help to save both of you from having an accident.

His sense of direction is as good as that of a compass, so that after a long ride, for example, he will be able to find the way home without any help.

Once you have learned to deal with a pony's way of doing things by understanding *why* he does them, you will find him kind, friendly, hard-working and always ready to join in fun and games.

Many ponies, such as the native breeds in Britain (e.g. Exmoor, Dartmoor and New Forest), still live in their wild state before they are rounded up and sold as riding ponies. The next book in this series, 'All Shapes and Sizes', tells you about the best-known breeds and types of pony.

In and around the circle are the first 8 books in the Compass Pony Guide series. Can you match the titles with the pictures?

1. MORE THAN JUST A PET 2. HEAD FIRST 3. BODYWORK 4. FORELEGS AND FOUR FEET 5. A BIT MORE THAN A MOUTH 6. TOP, TAIL AND OVERCOAT 7. FILLING UP THE TANK 8. WHY DOES HE DO THAT?